EXTRAORDINARY THINGS YOU DIDN'T KNOW ABOUT

FO⚽TBALL

PUBLISHER: SIMON MELHUISH

EDITOR: NIKOLE BAMFORD

COMPILER: PAUL LUCAS

DESIGN: STEPHEN GODSON

PUBLISHED BY: LAGOON BOOKS

PO BOX 311, KT2 5QW, UK

PO BOX 990915, BOSTON, MA 02199, USA

WWW.THELAGOONGROUP.COM

ISBN 978-1-90617-075-2

PRINTED IN CHINA.

EXTRAORDINARY THINGS YOU DIDN'T KNOW ABOUT FOOTBALL

THE MOST COMMON SURNAME AMONGST WORLD CUP PLAYERS IS GONZALES.

DIEGO MARADONA HAD HIS STOMACH STAPLED TO TRY AND LOSE WEIGHT.

JOSE MOURINHO HAS A DEGREE IN PHYSICAL EDUCATION.

COVENTRY CITY WAS THE FIRST ENGLISH PREMIER LEAGUE TEAM TO LAUNCH AN OFFICIAL CLUB ____. IN 1999.

SOUTH AFRICA HAS MORE REGISTERED FOOTBALL CLUBS THAN ANY OTHER COUNTRY (OVER 50,000).

THE BAYERN PART OF BAYERN MUNICH MEANS BAVARIA.

THE MASCOT OF THE LA GALAXY IS AN EXTRATERRESTRIAL FROG.

NORWICH CITY'S FOOTBALL SONG ON THE BALL, CITY IS REGARDED AS BEING THE OLDEST FOOTBALL SONG IN THE ENGLISH-SPEAKING WORLD.

SHEFFIELD WEDNESDAY ORIGINALLY STARTED OUT AS A CRICKET TEAM.

KEVIN KEEGAN'S NICKNAME WHILST HE WAS PLAYING IN GERMANY WAS MIGHTY MOUSE.

THE MINIMUM REST PERIOD BETWEEN TWO GAMES FOR ANY TEAM AT WORLD CUP MATCHES IS 48 HOURS, ACCORDING TO FIFA COMPETITION RULES.

ONLY ONE MANAGER HAD BEEN IN CHARGE OF THE ENGLAND INTERNATIONAL FOOTBALL TEAM BEFORE ALF RAMSEY.

STEVE MCMANAMAN IS THE ONLY ENGLISHMAN TO HAVE WON TWO CHAMPIONS LEAGUE TITLES.

ATHLETIC BILBAO DEFENDER ANDONI GOIKOETXEA BROKE MARADONA'S LEG IN FOUR PLACES IN A GAME AT THE NOU CAMP.

VINNIE JONES WAS SENT OFF IN ONLY HIS SECOND GAME FOR WALES IN 1995.

THE FIRST EUROPEAN TEAM TO WIN THE WORLD CUP WAS ITALY.

DIEGO MARADONA BECAME THE FIRST PRESIDENT OF THE INTERNATIONAL ASSOCIATION OF PROFESSIONAL FOOTBALLERS IN 1995.

ENGLISH PREMIER LEAGUE TEAM READING WAS ONCE KNOWN AS THE BISCUIT MEN.

ENGLISH PREMIER LEAGUE CLUB DERBY COUNTY SUPPOSEDLY ONCE SUFFERED (OR STILL DOES) FROM A GYPSY CURSE.

ENGLAND STAR STRIKER WAYNE ROONEY HAD MANY OF HIS CAPS STOLEN WHEN HIS HOUSE WAS BURGLED IN JULY 2006.

DAVID BECKHAM IS THE ONLY ENGLAND PLAYER TO HAVE BEEN SENT OFF TWICE DURING INTERNATIONALS.

ALAN BALL WAS THE YOUNGEST ENGLAND PLAYER ON THE PITCH FOR THE 1966 WORLD CUP FINAL.

GOALKEEPER DAVID SEAMAN PLAYED FOR ENGLAND AT LEAST ONCE EVERY YEAR FOR 15 CONSECUTIVE YEARS, A RECORD FOR ANY ENGLAND PLAYER.

IN SPAIN THE RICARDO ZAMORA TROPHY IS AWARDED ANNUALLY TO THE GOALKEEPER WHO HAS LET IN THE FEWEST GOALS IN THE SEASON.

THE FIRST FOOTBALLER TO WIN 100 ENGLAND CAPS WAS BILLY WRIGHT.

ITALIAN DEFENDER SANDRO SALVADORE SCORED TWO OWN GOALS IN THE SPACE OF THREE MINUTES IN THE 2-2 DRAW WITH SPAIN IN 1970.

THE FIRST PLAYER TO WIN THE PFA'S PLAYER OF THE YEAR AWARD FROM OUTSIDE THE UNITED KINGDOM WAS LIAM BRADY.

NO PLAYER HAS BEEN TRANSFERRED BETWEEN LIVERPOOL AND MANCHESTER UNITED SINCE 1964.

HUNGARY ONLY LOST ONE INTERNATIONAL BETWEEN 1950 AND 1956, THE MATCH BEING THE 1954 WORLD CUP FINAL.

ASTON VILLA FC HAS PROVIDED MORE ENGLAND INTERNATIONALS THAN ANY OTHER ENGLISH CLUB.

ENGLISH STRIKER IAN WRIGHT WAS SET TO BECOME A PLASTERER BEFORE HIS FOOTBALL CAREER TOOK OFF.

PETER CROUCH HOLDS THE RECORD FOR THE MOST ENGLAND GOALS IN ONE CALENDAR YEAR.

DAVID BECKHAM ASKED FOR THE NUMBER 23 SHIRT AT REAL MADRID BECAUSE IT WAS THE NUMBER SHIRT THAT MICHAEL JORDAN WORE.

WALTER NOVELLINO'S PLAYING CAREER WITH ITALY LASTED 45 MINUTES.

JUVENTUS'S ARENA, WHICH CAN HOLD WELL OVER 50,000 FANS, SAW JUST 237 SUPPORTERS TURN UP FOR A COPPA ITALIA GAME AGAINST SAMPDORIA IN THE 2001-2002 SEASON.

THE NAME OF THE FAN ON THE RECEIVING END OF ERIC CANTONA'S INFAMOUS KUNG-FU KICK WAS MATTHEW SIMMONS.

ARSENAL MANAGER ARSENE WENGER HAS A DEGREE IN ECONOMICS AND IS FLUENT IN ENGLISH, GERMAN AND FRENCH.

THE COUNTRY THAT HAS WON THE MOST OLYMPIC FOOTBALL GOLD MEDALS IS HUNGARY.

EMPOLI BOSS MARIO SOMMA IS FAMOUS FOR USING A SUBBUTEO SET TO HELP EXPLAIN HIS TACTICS.

TREVISO'S HOME STADIUM IS NAMED AFTER OMOBONO TENNI, A 1930S TT MOTORCYCLE CHAMPION.

ROBERTO BAGGIO WAS KNOWN AS IL DIVIN CODINO IN ITALY.

THE TEAM THAT HOLDS THE RECORD FOR THE FEWEST GOALS SCORED IN AN ENGLISH PREMIER LEAGUE SEASON (AS OF 2008) IS DERBY COUNTY.

RUUD VAN NISTELROOY CREATED AN ENGLISH LEAGUE RECORD IN JANUARY 2002 BY SCORING IN EIGHT CONSECUTIVE MATCHES.

IN 2001, CHELSEA FC BECAME THE FIRST TO PLAY AN ENGLISH PREMIER LEAGUE MATCH WITHOUT A SINGLE BRITISH-BORN PLAYER IN THEIR TEAM.

THE RULE DEMANDING GOALKEEPERS WEAR A DIFFERENT COLOUR SHIRT FROM THE REST OF THE TEAM WAS INTRODUCED IN 1913.

ACCORDING TO FIFA REGULATIONS, THE MAXIMUM CIRCUMFERENCE OF A MATCH FOOTBALL IS 70 CENTIMETRES (27.5 INCHES).

THE NEW ZEALAND FOOTBALL TEAM IS NICKNAMED THE ALL WHITES.

THERE ARE 208 MEMBER COUNTRIES IN FIFA AS OF 2008.

THE START OF THE 1974 WORLD CUP FINAL WAS DELAYED BECAUSE THERE WERE NO CORNER POSTS.

MANCHESTER UNITED'S CONTROVERSIAL STAR ERIC CANTONA PLAYED A FRENCH AMBASSADOR IN THE MOVIE ELIZABETH.

FORMER ARSENAL PLAYER PETER STOREY WAS JAILED FOR A VARIETY OF OFFENCES INCLUDING BROTHEL KEEPING AND FORGERY.

ARSENAL LEFT BACK SAMMY NELSON WAS CENSURED BY HIS CLUB FOR DROPPING HIS SHORTS IN A MATCH AGAINST COVENTRY IN 1979.

LORD RICHARD ATTENBOROUGH WAS ONCE A DIRECTOR OF CHELSEA FC.

THE GENERAL NAME GIVEN TO THE BEHIND-THE-SCENES STRUCTURE THAT BROUGHT LIVERPOOL SUCH CONTINUITY AND SUCCESS IN THE 1970S AND 1980S WAS THE BOOT ROOM BOYS.

GILLESPIE ROAD UNDERGROUND STATION CHANGED ITS NAME TO ARSENAL IN THE 1930S, AT THE REQUEST OF THE LOCAL FOOTBALL CLUB.

CAMEROON INTERNATIONAL MARC-VIVIEN FOE COLLAPSED AND DIED DURING A MATCH IN FRANCE IN 2003.

THE SCOTLAND TEAM TOOK TO THE FIELD IN 100-DEGREE HEAT IN SWITZERLAND IN 1954 WEARING WOOLLEN LONG-SLEEVED SHIRTS AND SUBSEQUENTLY LOST 7-0.

SCOTTISH INTERNATIONAL FOOTBALLER ALAN HANSEN ALSO REPRESENTED HIS COUNTRY AT SQUASH, VOLLEYBALL, BASKETBALL AND GOLF.

AC MILAN SUPPORTERS SANG YOU'LL NEVER WALK ALONE BEFORE THEIR 1989 EUROPEAN CUP SEMI-FINAL AGAINST REAL MADRID TO HONOUR THE 96 LIVERPOOL FC FANS KILLED IN THE HILLSBOROUGH TRAGEDY EARLIER IN THE SAME YEAR.

MATT HOLLAND, ALAN BRAZIL AND MIKE ENGLAND HAVE IN COMMON ALL PLAYED INTERNATIONAL FOOTBALL AGAINST THE COUNTRY OF THEIR SURNAME.

DAVID BECKHAM'S FULL NAME IS DAVID ROBERT JOSEPH BECKHAM.

UNTIL 2007, THE BALLON D'OR WAS AWARDED TO THE EUROPEAN FOOTBALLER OF THE YEAR. HOLLAND HAS PRODUCED THE MOST PLAYERS THAT HAVE WON BALLON D'OR AT LEAST THREE TIMES.

FORMER LIVERPOOL STRIKER MARK WALTERS'S MIDDLE NAME IS EVERTON.

THE CYPRIOT FOOTBALL TEAM WAS ALLOWED TO CHOOSE TO COMPETE IN EUROPE, ASIA OR AFRICA DUE TO ITS LOCATION.

ENGLAND'S 1966 WORLD CUP HAT-TRICK HERO GEOFF HURST ALSO PLAYED COUNTY CRICKET FOR ESSEX.

THERE IS A STATUE OF DAVID BECKHAM IN PARIWAS TEMPLE IN BANGKOK.

THE REAL IN REAL MADRID MEANS ROYAL.

FOOTBALLER DAVID GINOLA REPLACED PRINCESS DIANA IN THE INTERNATIONAL CAMPAIGN AGAINST LANDMINES.

ANDREI KANCHELSKIS IS THE ONLY PLAYER TO SCORE IN MANCHESTER, MERSEYSIDE AND GLASGOW DERBIES.

THE LARGEST CITY IN THE UK TO NEVER HAVE HAD A LEAGUE TEAM IS WAKEFIELD.

EIDUR GUDJOHNSEN WAS ONCE BROUGHT ON IN AN INTERNATIONAL MATCH AS A REPLACEMENT FOR HIS FATHER.

ERIC CANTONA WON THREE DIFFERENT LEAGUE CHAMPIONSHIPS WITH THREE DIFFERENT CLUBS IN THREE CONSECUTIVE YEARS.

IN ORDER TO ACHIEVE A GERMAN HAT-TRICK A PLAYER MUST SCORE THREE GOALS IN THE SAME HALF WITHOUT ANY GOALS BEING SCORED IN BETWEEN.

NUMBERS WERE FIRST PRINTED ON THE BACKS OF PLAYERS' SHIRTS ON 25TH AUGUST 1928.

A STAR ON A NATIONAL TEAM'S SHIRT SIGNIFIES A WORLD CUP WIN.

ENGLAND INTERNATIONAL DEFENDER SOL CAMPBELL'S REAL FIRST NAME IS SULZEER.

JULIO IGLESIAS PLAYED AS A GOALKEEPER FOR THE REAL MADRID YOUTH TEAM.

THE FIRST NORTH EUROPEAN TEAM OUTSIDE THE UK TO WIN A EUROPEAN CUP WAS FEYENOORD.

THE FIRST STADIUM IN EUROPE TO HAVE FLOODLIGHTS INSTALLED WAS BRAMALL LANE IN SHEFFIELD, UK.

WEST HAM UNITED WAS FORMERLY KNOWN AS THAMES IRONWORKS.

RANGERS HAVE WON MORE LEAGUE TITLES THAN ANY OTHER CLUB IN THE WORLD.

KEVIN KEEGAN IS THE ONLY ENGLISHMAN TO HAVE BEEN GIVEN THE BALLON D'OR TWICE.

SUNDERLAND FANS WERE FOUND TO BE THE LOUDEST IN A SURVEY CARRIED OUT AT EVERY ENGLISH LEAGUE GROUND.

BEFORE GOING INTO FOOTBALL MANAGEMENT, GÉRARD HOULLIER WAS A TEACHER.

CRISTIANO RONALDO WAS NAMED AFTER EX-US PRESIDENT RONALD REAGAN.

BIRMINGHAM CITY HAVE REACHED DOUBLE FIGURES IN A MATCH ON FIVE SEPARATE OCCASIONS.

PETER SHILTON IS THE ONLY PLAYER TO HAVE MADE OVER 1,000 ENGLISH LEAGUE APPEARANCES.

NEIL MCBAIN IS THE OLDEST EVER PLAYER TO PLAY IN THE ENGLISH LEAGUE, AT THE AGE OF 51 YEARS AND 120 DAYS.

DIDIER DROGBA WAS THE FIRST PLAYER TO BE SENT OFF IN A CHAMPIONS LEAGUE FINAL FOR VIOLENT CONDUCT.

FRANCESCO TOTTI'S MOTHER THREATENED TO CUT OFF HIS MANHOOD IF HE EVER LEFT ROMA.

SINGER ROBBIE WILLIAMS SUPPORTS PORT VALE.

IN THE 1971-72 SEASON, MANCHESTER CITY WERE AWARDED A STAGGERING 15 PENALTIES — ALL OF WHICH WERE SCORED BY FRANCIS LEE.

THE WORLD'S FIRST EVER INTERNATIONAL FOOTBALL MATCH WAS BETWEEN ENGLAND AND SCOTLAND IN 1872. IT ENDED AS A 0-0 DRAW.

THE WORLD CUP WAS STOLEN AFTER BEING PUT ON DISPLAY BY 1966 HOSTS ENGLAND. IT WAS LATER DISCOVERED BY A DOG CALLED PICKLES.

THE MEDITERRANEAN LEAGUE WAS FORMED IN 1937 DURING THE SPANISH CIVIL WAR. IT RAN FOR ONLY ONE COMPLETE SEASON, WITH BARCELONA RUNNING OUT CHAMPIONS.

PRIOR TO THE INTRODUCTION OF WHISTLES IN 1878, FOOTBALL REFEREES USED TO WAVE HANDKERCHIEFS WHEN AWARDING FREE KICKS.

BARCELONA FANS THREW A PIG'S HEAD AT THEIR FORMER FAVOURITE LUIS FIGO WHEN HE RETURNED TO THEIR GROUND PLAYING FOR REAL MADRID.

THE BEST GOALKEEPER OF THE WORLD CUP TOURNAMENT IS AWARDED THE LEV YASHIN AWARD.

THE FIRST RECORDED GAME OF STREET FOOTBALL WAS PLAYED AT SEDGEFIELD IN ENGLAND IN 1027.

ITALY LOST EIGHT OF THEIR INTERNATIONAL FIRST TEAM IN AN AIR CRASH IN 1949.

REFEREE ALMEIDA REGO BLEW THE FULL TIME WHISTLE SIX MINUTES EARLY DURING A WORLD CUP GAME IN THE 1930 TOURNAMENT.

THE GERMAN BUNDESLIGA WAS ONLY FORMED IN 1963, AFTER THE GERMAN NATIONAL SIDE'S POOR SHOWING AT THE 1962 WORLD CUP.

NOTTS COUNTY IS RECOGNISED AS THE OLDEST LEAGUE CLUB STILL IN EXISTENCE.

GERMANY BECAME THE FIRST NATION TO SUCCESSFULLY DEFEND A WOMEN'S WORLD CUP TITLE IN 2007, WHEN THEY BEAT BRAZIL 2-0 IN THE FINAL.

THE BRAZILIAN GOVERNMENT PROPOSED PUTTING A FOOTBALL ON THE NATIONAL FLAG OF BRAZIL IN THE 1970S.

SWITZERLAND ARE THE ONLY TEAM TO MISS ALL OF THEIR PENALTIES IN A WORLD CUP FINALS PENALTY SHOOT OUT (IN 2006).

CHELSEA WERE THE LAST WINNERS OF THE FA CUP AT THE OLD WEMBLEY STADIUM AND THE FIRST WINNERS AT THE NEW WEMBLEY STADIUM.

AJAX WERE THE FIRST WINNERS OF THE INTERTOTO CUP IN 1962.

ENGLAND CAPTAIN BOBBY MOORE WAS ARRESTED FOR SHOPLIFTING DURING THE 1970 WORLD CUP FINALS AND PLAYED IN THE TOURNAMENT WHILST RELEASED ON BAIL.

SAN MARINO'S ANDY SEVLA WAS THE MOST FOULED PLAYER DURING THE 2008 EUROPEAN CHAMPIONSHIPS QUALIFYING CAMPAIGN, BEING SINNED AGAINST 52 TIMES.

THIRTEEN PEOPLE DIED DURING A WORLD CUP QUALIFYING GAME BETWEEN ZIMBABWE AND SOUTH AFRICA IN 2000 AFTER POLICE FIRED TEAR GAS INTO THE CROWD.

IN 2007, SEVILLA BECAME THE FIRST CLUB TO SUCCESSFULLY DEFEND THEIR UEFA CUP TITLE SINCE REAL MADRID IN 1986.

BRAZIL IS THE ONLY TEAM TO HAVE COMPETED IN EVERY SINGLE WORLD CUP COMPETITION.

COVENTRY CITY WERE THE FIRST TEAM EVER TO TOP THE ENGLISH PREMIERSHIP, WHEN IT BEGAN IN 1992.

DURING THE SECOND WORLD WAR THE WORLD CUP TROPHY WAS HIDDEN UNDER THE BED OF AN ITALIAN FIFA VICE-PRESIDENT.

IF, DURING A SOCCER GAME, THE BALL HITS THE REFEREE AND ENDS UP IN THE BACK OF THE NET, THE GOAL STANDS.

EGYPT HAVE MADE 21 APPEARANCES AT THE AFRICA CUP OF NATIONS, MORE THAN ANY OTHER COUNTRY.

HOSTS SWITZERLAND WILL PLAY THE OPENING GAME OF THE 2008 EUROPEAN CHAMPIONSHIPS FINALS AGAINST THE CZECH REPUBLIC.

THE INTERTOTO CUP GETS ITS NAME FROM TOTO, THE GERMAN WORD FOR FOOTBALL POOLS.

A SWEDISH FILM MAKER MADE A DOCUMENTARY CLAIMING THAT THE 1958 WORLD CUP FINALS IN SWEDEN DIDN'T REALLY TAKE PLACE, BUT WERE STAGED BY AMERICAN AND SWEDISH TV COMPANIES.

ISRAEL WON THEIR 1958 WORLD CUP QUALIFYING GROUP WITHOUT PLAYING A MATCH, AFTER ALL THE OTHER TEAMS IN THEIR GROUP REFUSED TO PLAY.

WILLIAM KENYON-SLANEY SCORED ENGLAND'S FIRST EVER INTERNATIONAL GOAL, AGAINST SCOTLAND IN 1873.

DURING THE 1978 WORLD CUP, ARGENTINA'S STAR PLAYER OSSIE ARDILES WORE THE NUMBER 1 SHIRT.

ENGLAND STAR MICHAEL OWEN BECAME THE FIRST PLAYER TO SCORE INTERNATIONAL GOALS AT BOTH THE OLD WEMBLEY AND THE NEW WEMBLEY STADIUM WHEN HE NETTED IN 2007 IN THE GAME AGAINST ISRAEL.

NEW ZEALAND'S ONE AND ONLY APPEARANCE AT THE WORLD CUP FINALS CAME IN 1982.

THE FIRST HAT-TRICK IN THE ENGLISH PREMIERSHIP WAS SCORED BY ERIC CANTONA FOR LEEDS IN A 1992 GAME AGAINST TOTTENHAM.

IN 2014 BRAZIL WILL BECOME THE FIRST SOUTH AMERICAN COUNTRY TO HOST THE WORLD CUP TWICE.

SOVIET GOALKEEPER LEV YASHIN IS THE ONLY GOALKEEPER EVER TO HAVE WON THE EUROPEAN FOOTBALLER OF THE YEAR AWARD.

WHEN CHELSEA LOST TO TOTTENHAM IN THE 2008 CARLING CUP FINAL, IT WAS THE CLUB'S FIRST DEFEAT IN A FINAL SINCE NEW OWNER ROMAN ABRAMOVICH TOOK OVER IN 2003.

ENGLAND'S DAVID BECKHAM MISSED TWO PENALTIES AT THE EURO 2004 FINALS.

THE ONLY SIDE THAT FINISHED UNBEATEN AT THE 1974 WORLD CUP FINALS WAS SCOTLAND.

I NEVER COMMENT ON REFEREES, AND I'M NOT GOING TO BREAK THE HABIT OF A LIFETIME FOR THAT PRAT, REMARKED RON ATKINSON.

KING EDWARD II TRIED TO BAN STREET FOOTBALL IN ENGLAND IN 1314.

ARSENAL HAVE BEEN IN THE ENGLISH TOP FLIGHT FOR THE LONGEST CONSECUTIVE PERIOD.

THE 1994 WORLD CUP WAS THE FIRST TO BE DECIDED BY A PENALTY SHOOT OUT.

TONY ADAMS MISSED EIGHT WEEKS OF THE 1990-91 ENGLISH FOOTBALL SEASON AFTER HE WAS JAILED FOR DRINK DRIVING.

SWEDISH LEGEND GUNNAR NORDAHL SCORED AN INCREDIBLE 149 GOALS IN JUST 172 MATCHES IN THE SWEDISH LEAGUE, BEFORE MOVING TO AC MILAN WHERE HE HAD A 77% GOALS-TO-GAMES RATIO.

THE 2010 WORLD CUP IN SOUTH AFRICA WILL BE THE FIRST EVER HELD BY A NATION IN THE CONFEDERATION OF AFRICAN FOOTBALL.

SOUTH AFRICA ARE THE FIRST HOSTS SINCE 1934 TO PARTICIPATE IN THE WORLD CUP QUALIFIERS. THIS IS BECAUSE THE WORLD CUP QUALIFIERS ALSO SERVE AS THE QUALIFYING TOURNAMENT FOR THE 2010 AFRICAN CUP OF NATIONS.

BRAZIL WAS THE ONLY COUNTRY TO PUT FORWARD A BID TO HOST THE 2014 WORLD CUP.

THE OLDEST PLAYER EVER TO TAKE TO THE FIELD IN THE ENGLISH PREMIERSHIP IS JOHN BURRIDGE, WHO PLAYED IN GOAL FOR MANCHESTER CITY AT THE AGE OF 43 YEARS AND 162 DAYS.

THE 1986 WORLD CUP FINAL WAS THE FIRST ONE NOT PLAYED WITH A LEATHER BALL.

JUST THREE TEAMS PARTICIPATED IN THE FIRST EVER AFRICA CUP OF NATIONS IN 1957 – HOSTS SUDAN AND EGYPT AND ETHIOPIA.

THE FIRST FA CUP FINAL WAS PLAYED AT KENNINGTON OVAL CRICKET GROUND.

THE FIRST EVER WOMEN'S WORLD CUP WAS HELD IN CHINA IN 1991, AND WON BY THE USA.

GEOFF HURST WAS THE FIRST PLAYER TO SCORE WITH A HEADER IN A WORLD CUP FINAL IN 1966.

WHEN THE INTER-CITIES FAIRS CUP WAS REPLACED WITH THE UEFA CUP, THE TWO MOST SUCCESSFUL SIDES IN THE COMPETITION'S HISTORY MET IN A PLAY-OFF TO DECIDE WHO SHOULD KEEP THE TROPHY. BARCELONA BEAT LEEDS 2-1.

WEST GERMANY IS THE ONLY COUNTRY TO REACH THE FINAL OF THREE CONSECUTIVE WORLD CUPS.

THE TERM SOCCER COMES FROM A SLANG ABBREVIATION OF ASSOCIATION FOOTBALL.

HARALD SCHUMACHER, THE GERMAN GOALKEEPER WHO KNOCKED OUT TWO OF FRENCH PLAYER PATRICK BATTISTON'S TEETH WITH A HORRIBLE TACKLE IN THE 1982 WORLD CUP SEMI-FINAL, LATER WENT ON TO BECOME BEST MAN AT BATTISTON'S WEDDING.

LEGENDARY MANCHESTER UNITED MANAGER SIR MATT BUSBY SPENT EIGHT YEARS OF HIS PLAYING CAREER PLAYING FOR MANCHESTER CITY.

MANCHESTER CITY KEEPER BERT TRAUTMANN PLAYED THE LAST FIFTEEN MINUTES OF THE 1953 FA CUP FINAL WITH A BROKEN NECK.

THE FIRST EVER WORLD CUP MASCOT WAS WORLD CUP WILLIE — A LION, USED DURING THE 1966 FINALS IN ENGLAND.

THE FINAL OF THE 2004 EUROPEAN CHAMPIONSHIPS WAS A RE-MATCH OF THE OPENING GAME, BETWEEN PORTUGAL AND GREECE. ON BOTH OCCASIONS PORTUGAL LOST.

ARGENTINE PLAYER GABRIEL BATISTUTA WAS THE FIRST PLAYER TO SCORE HAT TRICKS AT THREE CONSECUTIVE WORLD CUP FINALS.

KEITH GILLESPIE WAS SENT OFF LESS THAN TEN SECONDS AFTER COMING ONTO THE PITCH IN THE ENGLISH PREMIERSHIP GAME BETWEEN SHEFFIELD UNITED AND READING IN 2007. THE BALL WAS NOT EVEN IN PLAY AT THE TIME HE ELBOWED READING'S STEPHEN HUNT, SO TECHNICALLY HE WAS SENT OFF AFTER 0 SECONDS.

BRAZIL'S REVOLUTIONARY 4-3-3 FORMATION AT THE 1962 WORLD CUP WAS NICKNAMED THE PENGUIN.

BRIAN CLOUGH ONCE SAID OF JOHN ROBERTSON 'HE'S A FAT DUMPY LAD WHO LIVES OUT OF A FRYING PAN, BUT GIVE HIM A BALL AND SOME GRASS AND HE BECOMES PICASSO'.

RYAN GIGGS HAS WON MORE HONOURS THAN ANY OTHER PLAYER IN THE ENGLISH LEAGUE.

ENGLAND AND MANCHESTER UNITED STAR WAYNE ROONEY SUFFERED THREE METATARSAL FRACTURES IN JUST FOUR YEARS.

BRAZILIAN JAIRZINHO IS THE ONLY PLAYER TO SCORE IN EVERY ROUND OF A WORLD CUP, INCLUDING THE FINAL.

COMMENTATOR THOMAS WOODROOFFE PLEDGED TO EAT HIS HAT IF A GOAL WAS SCORED IN THE 1938 FA CUP SHOWDOWN BETWEEN PRESTON AND HUDDERSFIELD. PRESTON'S GEORGE MUTCH ONLY NETTED FROM THE SPOT IN THE LAST MINUTE OF EXTRA TIME AND WOODROOFFE HAD TO TUCK IN.

THE FIRST ENGLISH PREMIERSHIP GOAL WAS SCORED BY BRIAN DEANE FOR SHEFFIELD UNITED, AGAINST MANCHESTER UNITED IN 1992.

DIANA ROSS MISSED A PENALTY WHILST PERFORMING IN THE OPENING CEREMONY OF THE 1994 WORLD CUP.

BRAZIL WERE THE FIRST TEAM TO BE ALLOWED TO KEEP THE WORLD CUP, AFTER WINNING IT FOR THE THIRD TIME IN 1970.

FRENCH PLAYER JUSTE FONTAINE HOLDS THE RECORD FOR THE MOST GOALS SCORED DURING A SINGLE WORLD CUP FINALS WITH THIRTEEN, SCORED AT THE 1958 FINALS.

THE 1976 EUROPEAN CHAMPIONSHIP FINAL BETWEEN WEST GERMANY AND CZECHOSLOVAKIA IS THE ONLY ONE THUS FAR THAT HAS BEEN DECIDED BY A PENALTY SHOOT OUT.

CAMEROON'S RIGOBERT SONG WAS SENT OFF IN TWO CONSECUTIVE WORLD CUP FINALS.

BRAZILIAN GENIUS GARRINCHA WAS NICKNAMED LITTLE BIRD.

RUSSIAN REFEREE VALENTIN VALENTINOVICH ISSUED A RECORD-BREAKING FOUR RED CARDS AND SIXTEEN YELLOW CARDS IN A SINGLE GAME BETWEEN PORTUGAL AND HOLLAND AT THE 2006 WORLD CUP FINALS.

PRIOR TO 1993, IF A CHARITY SHIELD FINAL WAS DRAWN EACH SIDE KEPT THE SHIELD FOR SIX MONTHS.

THE 1950 WORLD CUP FINALS WERE THE ONLY ONES IN WHICH NO PLAYER WAS SENT OFF.

THE FIRST RUSSIAN SIDE TO WIN ANY EUROPEAN COMPETITION WAS CSKA MOSCOW, WHO WON THE UEFA CUP IN 2005.

MEXICO WAS BANNED FROM THE 1990S WORLD CUP FINALS FOR FIELDING OVER-AGE PLAYERS AT A WORLD UNDER 20S TOURNAMENT.

ENGLISH REFEREE GRAHAM POLL MISTAKENLY BOOKED THE SAME PLAYER THREE TIMES IN A MATCH BETWEEN CROATIA AND AUSTRALIA AT THE 2006 WORLD CUP FINALS.

THE FOOTBALL CLICHÉ IT'S A FUNNY OLD GAME HAS BEEN ATTRIBUTED TO JIMMY GREAVES.

THE SMALLEST TOWN EVER TO WIN THE TOP DIVISION TITLE IN ENGLAND IS BURNLEY, IN 1921.

BRAZIL AND SWEDEN HAVE MET MORE TIMES AT WORLD CUP FINALS THAN ANY OTHER TWO TEAMS.

THE EUROPEAN CHAMPIONSHIP QUALIFYING MATCH BETWEEN SWEDEN AND DENMARK IN 2007 WAS ABANDONED IN THE 89TH MINUTE AFTER A DANISH FAN ATTACKED THE REFEREE. SWEDEN WERE AWARDED THE MATCH 3-0.

ARSENAL'S PAT RICE IS THE ONLY PLAYER TO HAVE APPEARED IN FIVE FA CUP FINALS WITH THE SAME CLUB.

THE 2002 WORLD CUP WAS THE FIRST TO BE HOSTED BY TWO SEPARATE COUNTRIES — SOUTH KOREA AND JAPAN.

SCOTTISH SIDE ABERDEEN'S GROUND IS CALLED PITTODRIE, WHICH MEANS PLACE OF MANURE.

THE 1994 WORLD CUP SAW THE FIRST EVER INDOOR MATCH, BETWEEN USA AND SWITZERLAND.

THE 1954 WORLD CUP FINAL, WHICH WEST GERMANY WON 3-2 AGAINST FAVOURITES HUNGARY, IS KNOWN IN GERMANY AS THE MIRACLE OF BERN.

PARTIZAN BELGRADE WERE DISQUALIFIED FROM THE 2007/2008 UEFA CUP AFTER THEIR MATCH IN MOSTAR WAS MARRED BY CROWD TROUBLE.

CARDIFF CITY WON THE 1927 FA CUP FINAL WITHOUT SCORING A GOAL – THE ONLY GOAL OF THE GAME WAS AN OWN-GOAL BY ARSENAL'S DAN LEWIS.

THE FIRST TEAM TO SCORE A WORLD CUP GOAL WAS FRANCE IN 1930.

CHILE WAS HIT BY THE LARGEST EARTHQUAKE OF THE TWENTIETH CENTURY JUST TWO YEARS BEFORE HOSTING THE 1962 WORLD CUP FINALS.

THE 1962 WORLD CUP MATCH BETWEEN CHILE AND ITALY BECAME KNOWN AS THE BATTLE OF SANTIAGO DUE TO THE HIGH NUMBER OF FOULS COMMITTED DURING THE GAME.

SWINDON ARE THE ONLY TEAM TO HAVE WON A PLAY-OFF FINAL BUT NOT GAIN PROMOTION TO THE TOP ENGLISH DIVISION. THE FA DENIED THEM PROMOTION AFTER THEY ADMITTED 36 BREACHES OF LEAGUE RULES.

LEGENDARY DANISH GOALKEEPER PETER SCHMEICHEL SCORED AN INCREDIBLE 11 GOALS IN HIS PLAYING CAREER.

BOB PAISLEY ONCE ADVISED HIS PLAYERS 'IF YOU'RE IN THE PENALTY AREA AND DON'T KNOW WHAT TO DO WITH THE BALL, PUT IT IN THE NET AND WE'LL DISCUSS THE OPTIONS LATER'.

WELSH STAR RYAN GIGGS WAS MADE AN MBE IN 2007.

JUVENTUS HAS LOST MORE CHAMPIONS LEAGUE/EUROPEAN CUP FINALS THAN ANY OTHER SIDE (5).

THIRTEEN TEAMS COMPETED IN THE FIRST WORLD CUP IN 1930.

BLACKPOOL LEGEND SIR STANLEY MATTHEWS ONCE WON AN FA CUP WINNER'S MEDAL AND A LONSDALE BOXING BELT IN THE SAME DAY. AFTER THE GAME HE WON THE BELT IN A RAFFLE AT A CHARITY DINNER.

CELTIC ARE THE ONLY SCOTTISH SIDE EVER TO HAVE WON THE EUROPEAN CUP.

WESTERN SAMOA'S FIRST INTERNATIONAL MATCH AGAINST FIJI IN 1924 WAS PLAYED ON A PITCH WITH A TREE IN THE MIDDLE OF IT.

ZICO IS ONE OF THE FEW LEGENDARY BRAZILIAN PLAYERS NEVER TO PLAY IN A WORLD CUP WINNING SIDE.

'YOU CANNOT GUARANTEE A THING IN THIS GAME. ALL YOU CAN GUARANTEE IS DISAPPOINTMENT.' THAT WAS THE BLEAK ASSESSMENT OF FOOTBALL OFFERED BY GRAEME SOUNESS.

MANCHESTER UNITED MOVED TO OLD TRAFFORD BECAUSE THEIR PREVIOUS GROUND, BANK STREET, WAS REGULARLY CONTAMINATED WITH TOXIC FUMES FROM A NEARBY CHEMICAL FACTORY.

OVER 715 MILLION PEOPLE WATCHED THE 2006 WORLD CUP FINAL.

THE FIRST PLAYER TO SCORE 30 GOALS IN THE ENGLISH PREMIERSHIP WAS SUNDERLAND'S KEVIN PHILLIPS.

MANCHESTER UNITED ARE THE ONLY SIDE TO WIN THE FA CUP HAVING PLAYED TOP FLIGHT OPPOSITION IN EVERY ROUND (IN 1948).

THE WINNERS OF THE EURO 2004 TOURNAMENT, GREECE, WERE 150-1 OUTSIDERS GOING INTO THE FINALS.

'IF YOU PUT ALL THE GERMAN PLAYERS, EXCEPT KAHN, IN A SACK AND HIT IT, YOU WOULD GET SOMEONE WHO DESERVED IT' — FRANZ BECKENBAUER OFFERING CONSTRUCTIVE CRITICISM AFTER A DISAPPOINTING DISPLAY FROM THE GERMAN SIDE.

ANY TEAM THAT HAS WON THE CHAMPIONS LEAGUE/EUROPEAN CUP MORE THAN FIVE TIMES, OR THREE TIMES IN A ROW, IS ALLOWED TO WEAR UEFA'S SPECIAL BADGE OF HONOUR. REAL MADRID, AC MILAN, LIVERPOOL, AJAX AND BAYERN MUNICH ARE THE ONLY TEAMS TO HAVE THIS HONOUR.

PETER SHILTON IS ENGLAND'S MOST CAPPED PLAYER, WITH 125 CAPS.

TOTTENHAM HOTSPUR IS THE ONLY NON-LEAGUE TEAM EVER TO WIN THE FA CUP, IN 1901.

THE ONLY SEEDED TEAM NOT TO QUALIFY FOR THE 2008 EUROPEAN CHAMPIONSHIPS WAS ENGLAND.

COLOMBIAN PLAYER ANDRES ESCOBAR WAS ASSASSINATED AFTER SCORING AN OWN GOAL AGAINST HOSTS USA IN THE 1994 WORLD CUP.

DIEGO MARADONA WAS GIVEN A TWO YEAR SUSPENDED JAIL SENTENCE FOR SHOOTING A JOURNALIST WITH AN AIR GUN.

IN 1999, MANCHESTER UNITED'S JONATHAN GREENING PICKED UP A CHAMPIONS LEAGUE WINNERS' MEDAL DESPITE NOT PLAYING ONE SECOND OF EUROPEAN FOOTBALL.

BRAZILIAN STAR GARRINCHA DIED OF ALCOHOL POISONING.

ENGLAND MANAGER GLENN HODDLE WAS SACKED IN 1999 AFTER MAKING REMARKS WHICH SEEMED TO SUGGEST THAT DISABLED PEOPLE WERE BEING PUNISHED FOR THE SINS THEY HAD COMMITTED IN A PREVIOUS LIFE.

STAR AUSTRALIAN PLAYER ARCHIE THOMPSON SCORED A RECORD 13 GOALS IN A SINGLE WORLD CUP QUALIFYING MATCH AGAINST AMERICAN SAMOA.

THE FIRST FA CUP GOAL SCORED AT THE NEW WEMBLEY STADIUM CAME IN THE 2007 FINAL AND WAS SCORED BY DIDIER DROGBA FOR CHELSEA.

ANGRY DUTCH FANS BOUGHT THEIR MANAGER DICK ADVOCAAT A FLIGHT HOME AFTER THEIR TEAM'S DISAPPOINTING PERFORMANCE AT THE 2004 EUROPEAN CHAMPIONSHIPS.

HEAVYWEIGHT BOXING LEGEND JOE LOUIS WAS SIGNED AS A PLAYER FOR LIVERPOOL FC IN 1944, AS A PUBLICITY STUNT.

SILVIO PIOLA HOLDS THE RECORD FOR THE MOST GOALS SCORED IN ITALY'S SERIE A LEAGUE, WITH 274 GOALS IN 537 GAMES.

HONDURAS AND EL SALVADOR WENT TO WAR WITH ONE ANOTHER AFTER A QUALIFYING MATCH FOR THE 1970S WORLD CUP TOURNAMENT. THE ENSUING WAR CAME TO BE KNOWN AS THE FOOTBALL WAR.

THE MISSING OF CHANCES IS ONE OF THE MYSTERIES OF LIFE, ACCORDING TO SIR ALF RAMSEY.

RYAN GIGGS SCORED THE LAST EVER GOAL IN AN FA CUP SEMI-FINAL REPLAY.

ENGLAND STAR GARY LINEKER FINISHED HIS CAREER PLAYING AT JAPANESE CLUB NAGOYA GRAMPUS EIGHT.

BEFORE WINNING THE 2004 TOURNAMENT, GREECE HAD NEVER WON A GAME AT THE EUROPEAN CHAMPIONSHIPS.

PELE'S REAL NAME IS EDSON ARANTES DO NASCIMENTO.

IN THE 1933 FA CUP FINAL, THE EVERTON TEAM WORE THE NUMBERS 1–11 AND THE OPPOSING TEAM, MANCHESTER CITY, WORE THE NUMBERS 12–22.

SAMUEL ETO'O OF CAMEROON IS THE AFRICA CUP OF NATION'S HIGHEST GOAL SCORER, WITH 16 GOALS.

THE FIRST MANCHESTER DERBY MATCH WAS PLAYED IN 1881, WHEN ST. MARKS (LATER MANCHESTER CITY) LOST TO VISITORS NEWTON HEATH LYR (LATER MANCHESTER UNITED) 3-0.

PERUVIAN GOALKEEPER RAMON QUIROGA WAS BOOKED DURING THE 1978 WORLD CUP FINALS FOR FOULING A POLISH PLAYER – IN THE POLISH HALF.

FAMOUS ENGLAND GOALKEEPER GORDON BANKS CONTINUED TO PLAY PROFESSIONAL FOOTBALL IN THE USA AFTER LOSING THE SIGHT IN HIS RIGHT EYE.

THE 2004 EUROPEAN CHAMPIONSHIPS WERE THE ONLY ONES TO FEATURE THE SILVER GOAL RULE. THE LAST SILVER GOAL WAS SCORED BY GREECE TO KNOCK OUT THE CZECH REPUBLIC.

DAVID BECKHAM PAID TRIBUTE TO HIS PARENTS, STATING THAT 'THEY HAD BEEN THERE FOR ME, EVER SINCE I WAS ABOUT SEVEN'.

THE ONLY TWO PLAYERS TO HAVE WON THE FIFA WORLD PLAYER OF THE YEAR AWARD THREE TIMES ARE ZINEDINE ZIDANE AND RONALDO.

THE WEST HAM UNITED SIDE OF 1975 WAS THE LAST ALL-ENGLISH SIDE TO LIFT THE FA CUP.

THE TINY NATION OF DUTCH EAST INDIES QUALIFIED FOR THE 1938 WORLD CUP FINALS.

SWISS TEAM SERVETTE FC WERE THE WINNERS OF THE EARLIEST RECOGNISED INTERNATIONAL FOOTBALL TOURNAMENT, THE TORNEO INTERNAZIONAL STAMPA SPORTIVA IN 1908.

THE MYSTERIOUS DWARFS, VENOMOUS VIPERS AND HEARTS OF OAK ALL PLAY IN THE FIRST DIVISION IN GHANA.

SIXTEEN AFRICAN NATIONS BOYCOTTED THE 1966 WORLD CUP FINALS IN PROTEST AT THE RULES OF QUALIFICATION FOR AFRICAN NATIONS.

STANLEY MATTHEWS WAS STILL PLAYING PROFESSIONALLY AT THE AGE OF 50.

BOB CHATT OF ASTON VILLA SCORED THE FASTEST EVER FA CUP FINAL GOAL AFTER JUST 30 SECONDS OF THE 1895 FINAL.

ONLY SEVEN NATIONS HAVE EVER WON THE WORLD CUP – BRAZIL, ITALY, GERMANY, URUGUAY, ARGENTINA, ENGLAND AND FRANCE.

IN 2006 THE CONFEDERATION OF AFRICAN FOOTBALL DECIDED FOR THE FIRST TIME TO REVEAL THE HOSTS FOR THE NEXT THREE AFRICA CUP OF NATIONS TOURNAMENTS. ANGOLA, GABON AND EQUATORIAL GUINEA AND LIBYA WILL HOST THE 2010, 2012 AND 2014 TOURNAMENTS.

SPURS KEEPER PAT JENNINGS SCORED FROM WITHIN HIS OWN PENALTY AREA IN THE 1967 CHARITY SHIELD FINAL.

THIERRY HENRY ONCE WISELY NOTED THAT 'SOMETIMES IN FOOTBALL YOU HAVE TO SCORE GOALS'.

ABERDEEN FC'S TRAINER DONALD COLMAN INVENTED THE DUG-OUT IN THE 1920S.

THE 1950 CHARITY SHIELD FINAL WAS PLAYED BETWEEN ENGLAND'S WORLD CUP SQUAD AND A CANADIAN TOURING TEAM.

THE FIRST FOREIGN PLAYER TO PLAY IN THE ENGLISH TOP DIVISION WAS CANADIAN WALTER BOWMAN IN 1892.

THE RECORD NUMBER OF ENTRIES FOR THE FA CUP IS 661 TEAMS IN 2004.

WALES AND LIVERPOOL STRIKER IAN RUSH CLAIMED HE RETURNED TO ENGLAND BECAUSE PLAYING IN ITALY WAS LIKE LIVING IN A FOREIGN COUNTRY.

ARGENTINE FORWARD BERNABE FERREYRA SCORED AT A RATE OF MORE THAN A GOAL A GAME, AND WAS CONSIDERED SO LETHAL THAT THE NEWSPAPER CRITICA OFFERED A PRIZE TO THE FIRST GOALKEEPER THAT COULD KEEP A CLEAN SHEET AGAINST HIM.

GOALKEEPER DAVE BEASANT WAS OUT OF ACTION FOR TWO MONTHS AFTER HE RUPTURED HIS ANKLE LIGAMENTS BY DROPPING A BOTTLE OF SALAD CREAM ON HIS FOOT.

THE MOST PROLIFIC SCORER IN BRITISH FOOTBALL HISTORY IS JIMMY MCGRORY, WHO SCORED 550 TIMES IN FIRST CLASS MATCHES.

ENGLAND LEGEND STUART PEARCE ONCE CLAIMED HE COULD 'SEE THE CARROT AT THE END OF THE TUNNEL'.

REAL MADRID COMPETED IN FIFTEEN CONSECUTIVE CHAMPIONS' CUP COMPETITIONS BETWEEN 1955/56 AND 1969/70.

THE FIRST EVER GOLDEN GOAL IN A EUROPEAN CHAMPIONSHIP WAS SCORED BY GERMANY IN THE 1996 FINAL AGAINST THE CZECH REPUBLIC.

ECUADORIAN PLAYER ATA VALENCIA WAS SENT OFF IN 1996 BEFORE EVEN MAKING IT ONTO THE PITCH.

KENNETH WOLSTENHOLME, THE BBC COMMENTATOR ON THE 1966 WORLD CUP FINAL WHOSE QUOTE 'THEY THINK IT'S ALL OVER – IT IS NOW' BECAME FAMOUS, WAS AWARDED THE DISTINGUISHED FLYING CROSS FOR HIS RAF SERVICE DURING WORLD WAR II.

PELE'S FAMILY NICKNAMED HIM DICO.

THE RULES OF THE CHARITY SHIELD WERE CHANGED IN 1974, WHEN THE FA CUP HOLDERS PLAYED THE REIGNING LEAGUE CHAMPIONS FOR THE FIRST TIME.

THE UK PRIME MINISTER GORDON BROWN ONCE SOLD FOOTBALL PROGRAMMES OUTSIDE SCOTTISH SIDE RAITH ROVERS' GROUND.

ACCORDING TO FIFA, ASSISTANT REFEREES RUN FOUR MILES IN THE AVERAGE GAME.

IN 1975, FOOTBALL AUTHORITIES CONSIDERED BANNING FOOTBALLERS FROM HUGGING EACH OTHER.

SKONTO RIGA HOLD THE RECORD FOR WINNING THE MOST CONSECUTIVE DOMESTIC LEAGUE TITLES. THEY TOPPED THE LATVIAN LEAGUE FOR 14 YEARS IN A ROW FROM 1991.

AFTER RAITH ROVERS DEFEATED THE MIGHTY CELTIC IN THE 1995 SCOTTISH LEAGUE CUP, RAITH MANAGER JIMMY NICHOLL SAID 'THIS WOULD BRING A TEAR TO A GLASS EYE'.

THE 1938 FINAL BETWEEN PRESTON NORTH END AND HUDDERSFIELD WAS THE FIRST FA CUP FINAL TO BE TELEVISED LIVE.

THE FIRST PLAYER TO SCORE IN A FIFA SANCTIONED MATCH AT THE NEW WEMBLEY STADIUM IN ENGLAND WAS ITALIAN STRIKER GIAMPAOLO PAZZINI IN 2007.

NORWEGIAN DEFENDER SVEIN GRONDALEN MISSED A KEY INTERNATIONAL MATCH AFTER COLLIDING WITH A MOOSE WHILST JOGGING.

AS OF 2007, 42 DIFFERENT SIDES HAVE WON THE FA CUP.

SHERLOCK HOLMES CREATOR SIR ARTHUR CONAN DOYLE WAS ONE OF THE CO-FOUNDERS OF PORTSMOUTH FOOTBALL CLUB.

LIVERPOOL'S FAMOUS KOP STAND IS NAMED AFTER A BATTLE IN THE BOER WAR.

LEGENDARY CHELSEA GOALKEEPER WILLIAM FOULKE WAS 6FT 7IN/2.01M TALL AND WEIGHED AROUND 24 STONE. PERHAPS NOT SURPRISINGLY HE WAS NICKNAMED FATTY.

ALVECHURCH AND OXFORD PLAYED EACH OTHER SIX TIMES IN THE 1971 FA CUP, BEFORE ALVECHURCH FINALLY TRIUMPHED.

THE RECORD FOR THE HIGHEST NUMBER OF GOALS SCORED BY ANY ONE PLAYER DURING A EUROPEAN CHAMPIONSHIP QUALIFYING CAMPAIGN IS HELD BY NORTHERN IRELAND'S DAVID HEALY, WHO SCORED 13 TIMES DURING THE 2008 CAMPAIGN. DESPITE THIS, NORTHERN IRELAND FAILED TO QUALIFY.

AS OF DECEMBER 2007, GERMANY ARE THE TOP-RANKED WOMEN'S FOOTBALL TEAM.

IN A RECENT SURVEY, 40% OF CROATIAN MEN SAID THEY WOULD RATHER WATCH THEIR NATIONAL TEAM PLAY THAN GO ON A DATE WITH ANGELINA JOLIE.

THE ONLY TIME EAST GERMANY PLAYED WEST GERMANY AT A WORLD CUP FINALS, THE GAME ENDED 1-0 TO EAST GERMANY.

THE ARCH AT THE NEW WEMBLEY STADIUM IS AS HEAVY AS TEN JUMBO JETS.

ASTON VILLA DEFENDER CHRIS NICHOLL SCORED ALL FOUR GOALS IN HIS SIDE'S 2-2 DRAW WITH LEICESTER CITY IN 1976.

BOBBY MOORE IS ENGLAND'S MOST CAPPED OUTFIELD PLAYER WITH 108 CAPS.

THE 1963 FA CUP FINAL HAD TO BE MOVED BACK BY THREE WEEKS DUE TO A SEVERE WINTER.

THE EUROPEAN CHAMPIONSHIPS WERE ORIGINALLY CALLED THE EUROPEAN NATIONS CUP.

STEVE MORROW BROKE HIS ARM WHEN HE WAS DROPPED BY TEAM MATE TONY ADAMS DURING ARSENAL'S CELEBRATIONS AFTER WINNING THE 1993 LITTLEWOODS CUP.

GEORGE BEST CONFESSED 'I SPENT A LOT OF MY MONEY ON BOOZE, BIRDS AND FAST CARS. THE REST I JUST SQUANDERED'.

LIVERPOOL FC'S ORIGINAL NAME WAS EVERTON FC. THEY HAD TO CHANGE IT AFTER THE FA REFUSED TO RECOGNISE THE TEAM AS EVERTON.

DIDIER DROGBA HAS A BEER NAMED AFTER HIM IN HIS NATIVE COUNTRY, IVORY COAST.

THE BIGGEST WIN IN FA CUP FINAL HISTORY CAME IN 1903 WHEN BURY BEAT DERBY COUNTY 6-0.

THE FIRST SIDE TO BEAT ENGLAND AT THEIR HOME GROUND OF WEMBLEY WAS HUNGARY.

THE OFFICIAL NAME OF MILAN'S SAN SIRO STADIUM IS STADIO GIUSEPPE MEAZZA, AND IT IS NAMED AFTER THE ITALIAN 1930S STRIKER WHO SCORED 243 GOALS FOR INTER.

KEVIN MORAN OF MANCHESTER UNITED BECAME THE FIRST PLAYER EVER TO BE SENT OFF IN AN FA CUP FINAL IN 1985.

AS OF 2008, ZINEDINE ZIDANE IS THE MOST EXPENSIVE PLAYER EVER SIGNED, LEAVING JUVENTUS FOR REAL MADRID FOR A REPORTED £46 MILLION (AROUND $90 MILLION).

SCOTTISH SIDE GLASGOW RANGERS ARE NAMED AFTER AN ENGLISH RUGBY TEAM.

IN THE 1984 EUROPEAN CHAMPIONSHIP TOURNAMENT FRANCE'S MICHEL PLATINI SCORED NINE GOALS IN JUST FIVE GAMES.

IN THE 1930S, THE CREWE AND DERBY RAILWAY VETERANS ASSOCIATIONS PLAYED AN ANNUAL GAME OF FOOTBALL AT WALKING PACE. ALL THE PLAYERS WERE OVER THE AGE OF 65.

DAVID BECKHAM WAS ON LOAN AT PRESTON NORTH END BEFORE SECURING A REGULAR PLACE IN THE MANCHESTER UNITED TEAM.

WELSH PLAYER JOHN CHARLES, RATED BY MANY AS THE BEST BRITISH PLAYER OF ALL TIME, WAS NEVER BOOKED IN HIS 537 PROFESSIONAL APPEARANCES.

THE GROUNDS OF SCOTTISH SIDES DUNDEE AND DUNDEE UNITED ARE JUST 50 YARDS APART.

LIVERPOOL STRIKER ALBERT STUBBINS FEATURES ON THE FAMOUS BEATLES ALBUM COVER SGT PEPPER'S LONELY HEARTS CLUB BAND.

THE 2000 AFRICA CUP OF NATIONS TOURNAMENT WAS DUE TO BE HELD IN ZIMBABWE, BUT THEY WERE FOUND NOT TO HAVE PROPERLY PREPARED FOR THE EVENT AND SO GHANA AND NIGERIA CO-HOSTED IT INSTEAD.

IN THE WINTER OF 1963, BLACKPOOL FC USED A FLAMETHROWER TO THAW THEIR PITCH.

ROB RESENBRINK SCORED THE 1000TH WORLD CUP GOAL FOR HOLLAND IN A MATCH AGAINST SCOTLAND AT THE 1978 WORLD CUP FINALS IN ARGENTINA.

IN THE EARLY DAYS OF FOOTBALL PLAYERS WERE OFTEN GIVEN FLORINS TO HOLD TO STOP THEM HANDLING THE BALL.

THE FIRST AFRICAN TEAM TO WIN A MATCH AT A WORLD CUP FINALS WAS TUNISIA. THEY BEAT MEXICO 3-1 IN 1978.

FULHAM AND ENGLAND MIDFIELDER JOHNNY HAYNES WAS CALLED THE FIRST FOOTBALL SUPERSTAR AND BECAME THE FIRST PLAYER EVER TO EARN MORE THAN £100 A WEEK WHEN THE MAXIMUM WAGE WAS ABOLISHED IN THE UK IN 1961.

WANDERERS, THE WINNERS OF THE FIRST FA CUP FINAL, WERE NOT AWARDED THE TROPHY ON THE DAY. INSTEAD THE PRESENTATION TOOK PLACE AT THEIR ANNUAL AWARDS DINNER, THREE WEEKS LATER.

THE PLAYERS OF THE UNITED ARAB EMIRATES WERE PROMISED A ROLLS ROYCE FOR EVERY GOAL THEY SCORED IN THE 1990 WORLD CUP FINALS.

HUNGARY'S LAST APPEARANCE AT A EUROPEAN CHAMPIONSHIP WAS BACK IN 1972.

LEEDS UNITED WERE DOCKED A MASSIVE 15 POINTS AT THE START OF THE 2007/2008 SEASON AFTER BRIEFLY GOING INTO ADMINISTRATION.

ZINEDINE ZIDANE CAME TOP OF UEFA'S GOLDEN JUBILEE POLL TO SELECT THE BEST EUROPEAN PLAYER OF THE LAST FIFTY YEARS.

WHEN INFORMED THAT ONE OF HIS STRIKERS HAD CONCUSSION AND DIDN'T KNOW WHO HE WAS, PARTICK THISTLE MANAGER JOHN LAMBIE IS REPORTED TO HAVE SAID 'THAT'S GREAT — TELL HIM HE'S PELE AND GET HIM BACK ON'.

THE 1954 WORLD CUP FINAL WAS HELD AT THE WANKDORF STADIUM.

MADAGASCAN SIDE STADE OLYMPIQUE DE L'EMRYNE ONCE SCORED 149 OWN GOALS IN A SINGLE GAME IN 2002. THEY WERE PROTESTING AT A SERIES OF CONTROVERSIAL REFEREEING DECISIONS.

DUTCH GENIUS JOHAN CRUIJFF ONCE SCORED A PENALTY BY PASSING THE BALL FROM THE PENALTY SPOT TO A TEAM-MATE, WHO PASSED IT BACK TO HIM BEFORE CRUIJFF PUT IT IN THE NET.

SCOTTISH SIDE QUEEN'S PARK REACHED TWO FA CUP FINALS IN THE NINETEENTH CENTURY.

THE LAST TIME NEITHER GERMANY NOR BRAZIL MADE IT AT LEAST AS FAR AS THE SEMI-FINALS OF THE WORLD CUP WAS 1930.

ARSENAL LEGEND CHARLIE GEORGE HAD ONE OF HIS FINGERS CUT OFF IN A LAWNMOWER ACCIDENT LATE ON IN HIS CAREER.

WILFRED MINTER SCORED NO FEWER THAN SEVEN GOALS FOR ST ALBANS CITY IN A 1922 MATCH AGAINST DULWICH HAMLET. BUT CITY LOST 8-7!

THE 1998 AFRICA CUP OF NATIONS IN BURKINA FASO PRODUCED 93 GOALS IN JUST 32 GAMES.

THE BIGGEST WIN FOR ANY TEAM IN THE CURRENT CHAMPIONS LEAGUE FORMAT CAME IN 2007, WHEN LIVERPOOL BEAT BESIKTAS 8-0 AT ANFIELD.

ITALIAN STAR STRIKER PAOLO ROSSI WAS BANNED FROM PLAYING FOR TWO YEARS AFTER BEING FOUND GUILTY OF BEING INVOLVED IN A BRIBERY CASE.

THE 1968 EUROPEAN CHAMPIONSHIP SEMI-FINAL BETWEEN ITALY AND THE USSR WAS DECIDED ON A COIN TOSS (WHICH ITALY WON).

THE FIFA 100 LIST OF ALL-TIME GREAT PLAYERS WAS COMPILED BY PELE IN 2004, AND INCLUDES 125 NAMES AS PELE FOUND IT TOO DIFFICULT TO CHOOSE JUST 100.

LUIS MONTI IS THE ONLY PLAYER EVER TO PLAY IN THE WORLD CUP FINALS FOR TWO DIFFERENT COUNTRIES — ARGENTINA AND ITALY.

THE FIRST AFRICAN PLAYER TO WIN FIFA WORLD FOOTBALLER OF THE YEAR WAS GEORGE WEAH.

STAR FEMALE USA STRIKER MIA HAMM SCORED MORE INTERNATIONAL GOALS IN HER CAREER THAN ANY OTHER PLAYER (MALE OR FEMALE).

THE QUEEN LAST ATTENDED AN FA CUP FINAL IN 1976.

THE FIRST OCCASION ON WHICH TWO PLAYERS ON OPPOSING SIDES BOTH SCORED HAT-TRICKS IN THE SAME ENGLISH PREMIERSHIP GAME WAS THE WIGAN V BLACKBURN GAME IN DECEMBER 2007 (SANTA CRUZ FOR BLACKBURN AND BENT FOR WIGAN).

THE URUGUAYAN PLAYER CASTRO, WHO PLAYED IN THE 1930S WORLD CUP TOURNAMENTS, HAD ONLY ONE ARM.

MAHMOUD EL-GOHARY OF EGYPT IS THE ONLY PERSON TO HAVE WON THE AFRICA CUP OF NATIONS AS BOTH A PLAYER AND A COACH (IN 1959 AND 1998).

THE RECORD FOR THE MOST APPEARANCES FOR A SINGLE CLUB IN THE ENGLISH LEAGUE IS HELD BY JOHN TROLLOPE, WHO PLAYED 770 TIMES FOR LUTON TOWN.

BRENTFORD'S GRIFFIN PARK GROUND IS THE ONLY ENGLISH LEAGUE GROUND TO HAVE A PUB ON EVERY CORNER.

SAUDI ARABIA IS THE ONLY COUNTRY EVER TO FIRE ITS COACH HALFWAY THROUGH A WORLD CUP TOURNAMENT FINAL.

NEITHER CELTIC NOR RANGERS, BOTH FOUNDER MEMBERS OF THE SCOTTISH LEAGUE, HAVE EVER BEEN RELEGATED.

ROGER LEMERRE, SACKED AS FRANCE'S TEAM COACH AFTER THEIR DISAPPOINTING EARLY EXIT FROM THE 2002 WORLD CUP, TOOK UP A POST AS TUNISIA'S MANAGER AND LED THEM TO AFRICA CUP OF NATIONS VICTORY IN 2004.

LOTHAR MATTHAUS IS THE MOST CAPPED GERMAN PLAYER OF ALL TIME, AND WAS THE FIRST EVER WINNER OF THE FIFA WORLD PLAYER OF THE YEAR AWARD IN 1991.

LIVERPOOL'S IAN RUSH HAS SCORED THE MOST GOALS IN FA CUP FINAL MATCHES — FIVE.

THE LARGEST CROWD THAT HAS EVER WATCHED AN INTERNATIONAL UNDER 21 MATCH GATHERED AT WEMBLEY STADIUM IN 2007. THE 55,700 SPECTATORS SAW ENGLAND UNDER 21S DRAW WITH ITALY UNDER 21S 3-3.

PORTUGAL'S BEST EVER GOALKEEPER, VITOR BAIA, WAS ADVISED TO QUIT THE GAME AGED JUST SIXTEEN AFTER SERIOUSLY INJURING HIS ARM.

THE 1966 WORLD CUP TOURNAMENT DRAW WAS THE FIRST TO BE TELEVISED LIVE.

THE TWELVE FOUNDING TEAMS OF THE FIRST EVER FOOTBALL LEAGUE (ENGLAND, 1888) WERE ACCRINGTON, ASTON VILLA, BLACKBURN ROVERS, BOLTON WANDERERS, BURNLEY, DERBY COUNTY, EVERTON, NOTTS COUNTY, PRESTON NORTH END, STOKE, WEST BROMWICH ALBION AND WOLVERHAMPTON WANDERERS.

EGYPT WERE THE FIRST AFRICAN TEAM TO COMPETE IN THE WORLD CUP, IN 1934.

ITALIAN GOALKEEPER WALTER ZENGA WENT 517 MINUTES WITHOUT CONCEDING A GOAL IN THE 1990 WORLD CUP FINALS.

98,000 PEOPLE CRAMMED INTO WEMBLEY STADIUM TO WATCH THE 1966 WORLD CUP FINAL BETWEEN ENGLAND AND WEST GERMANY.

THE OFFICIAL SOCCER RULE BOOK PUBLISHED BY THE INTERNATIONAL FOOTBALL ASSOCIATION BOARD IS JUST 50 PAGES LONG AND CONTAINS ONLY 17 RULES.

REGINALD ERSKINE 'TIP' FOSTER IS THE ONLY MAN TO HAVE EVER CAPTAINED ENGLAND AT BOTH FOOTBALL AND CRICKET.

THE ORIGINAL JULES RIMET WORLD CUP TROPHY WAS GIVEN TO BRAZIL TO KEEP, BUT WAS STOLEN AND MELTED DOWN FOR ITS GOLD CONTENT.

CAMEROON'S PLAYERS WERE BANNED FROM WEARING SLEEVELESS SHIRTS AT THE 2002 WORLD CUP FINALS.

IRISH KEEPER PADDY KENNY HAD AN EYEBROW BITTEN OFF IN A DRUNKEN BRAWL IN A HALIFAX CURRY SHOP IN 2006.

NORMAN HUNTER WAS NICKNAMED 'BITE YER LEGS' FOR HIS AGGRESSIVE STYLE OF PLAY.

GERMANY/WEST GERMANY ARE THE ONLY TEAM TO HAVE WON THREE EUROPEAN CHAMPIONSHIPS.

THE RECORD FOR THE BIGGEST WIN IN A WORLD CUP QUALIFYING GAME IS HELD BY AUSTRALIA, WHO BEAT AMERICAN SAMOA 31-0 IN A 2001 MATCH.

A STANDARD GOAL MEASURES 8 FEET HIGH BY 8 YARDS WIDE (2.44M HIGH BY 7.32 METRES WIDE).

ENGLAND'S FIRST EVER CAPTAIN AT A WORLD CUP FINALS WAS BILLY WRIGHT.

THE MEDIEVAL GAME OF SHROVETIDE FOOTBALL WAS PLAYED WITH A HOG'S HEAD OR INFLATED SHEEP'S BLADDER AS A BALL.

THE 1994 WORLD CUP FINALS WERE THE FIRST WHICH FEATURED THE PLAYERS' NAMES ON THE BACKS OF THEIR SHIRTS.

BLACKPOOL'S STAN MORTENSEN WAS THE LAST PLAYER TO SCORE A HAT-TRICK IN AN FA CUP FINAL BACK IN 1953.

THE 2008 UEFA INTERTOTO CUP CAMPAIGN WAS THE LAST EVER PLAYED.

YUGOSLAVIA PLAYED A WORLD CUP MATCH WITH TEN MEN AGAINST BRAZIL IN 1970 AFTER ONE OF THEIR PLAYERS KNOCKED THEMSELVES OUT WHILST RUNNING ONTO THE PITCH. IN THOSE DAYS, SUBSTITUTES WERE NOT ALLOWED.

IN 2002 CAMEROON BECAME THE FIRST SIDE TO WIN THE AFRICA CUP OF NATIONS WITHOUT CONCEDING A SINGLE GOAL IN NORMAL TIME.

THE REPUBLIC OF IRELAND REACHED THE QUARTER FINALS OF THE 1990 WORLD CUP WITHOUT WINNING A SINGLE GAME IN NORMAL TIME.

THE OFFICIAL ATTENDANCE AT THE FIRST EVER WEMBLEY FA CUP FINAL WAS 126,047.

THE FIRST CHARITY SHIELD MATCH BETWEEN MANCHESTER UNITED AND QUEENS PARK RANGERS ENDED 1-1, LEADING TO THE ONLY REPLAY IN THE HISTORY OF THE CHARITY SHIELD (WHICH UNITED WON 4-0).

FRENCH DEFENDER LAURENT BLANC KISSED THE BALD HEAD OF GOALKEEPER FABIEN BARTHEZ FOR GOOD LUCK BEFORE EVERY GAME OF THE 1998 WORLD CUP FINALS.

NEWCASTLE UNITED IS THE ONLY TEAM TO HAVE PROGRESSED PAST THE GROUP STAGES OF THE CHAMPIONS LEAGUE AFTER HAVING LOST THEIR FIRST THREE GAMES.

THE 1962 WORLD CUP FINALS WERE THE LAST ONES NOT TO BE BROADCAST LIVE IN EUROPE.

THE BIGGEST WIN IN EUROPEAN CHAMPIONSHIP QUALIFYING HISTORY WAS GERMANY'S 13-0 VICTORY AWAY TO SAN MARINO IN 2006.

ARGENTINE GOALKEEPER SERGIO GOYCOCHEA URINATED ON THE PITCH BEFORE EACH PENALTY SHOOT OUT IN THE 1990 WORLD CUP FINALS. HE SAVED A TOTAL OF FIVE PENALTIES.

MANCHESTER CITY FINISHED THEIR 1906 GAME AGAINST ARSENAL WITH JUST SIX PLAYERS, AS THE OTHERS HAD COLLAPSED FROM HEAT STROKE.

LEGENDARY PORTUGUESE STRIKER EUSEBIO WAS BORN IN MOZAMBIQUE.

EBENEZER COBB MORLEY IS KNOWN AS THE FATHER OF FOOTBALL FOR DRAFTING THE FIRST LAWS OF THE GAME IN HIS LONDON HOME.

THE ENTIRE ROMANIAN TEAM BLEACHED THEIR HAIR TO CELEBRATE REACHING THE SECOND ROUND OF THE 1998 WORLD CUP FINALS.

THE FIRST BLACK PLAYER TO PLAY FOR ENGLAND WAS VIV ANDERSON.

THE FIRST EVER FA TROPHY WAS STOLEN AND NEVER RECOVERED.

OLEG SALENKO OF RUSSIA BECAME THE FIRST MAN TO SCORE FIVE GOALS IN A SINGLE WORLD CUP GAME AGAINST CAMEROON IN 1994.

CHILE WAS DISQUALIFIED FROM THE 1990 WORLD CUP FINALS BECAUSE THEIR GOALKEEPER FEIGNED INJURY AFTER A FIREWORK WAS THROWN FROM THE STANDS.

RYAN GIGGS' DAD, DANNY WILSON, WAS A TOP RUGBY LEAGUE PLAYER.

THE ONLY PLAYER TO HAVE SCORED HAT-TRICKS IN ALL FOUR ENGLISH DIVISIONS, THE FA CUP, THE LEAGUE CUP, AND AT INTERNATIONAL LEVEL IS WALES' ROBERT EARNSHAW.

STANLEY MATTHEWS' NICKNAME WAS THE WIZARD OF DRIBBLE.

PELE MADE HIS WORLD CUP DEBUT IN 1958, PLAYING IN BRAZIL'S LAST GROUP GAME.

WALES MADE THEIR ONLY WORLD CUP APPEARANCE IN 1958 — THEY WERE KNOCKED OUT AFTER THE GROUP STAGES BY BRAZIL.

DANIEL AMOKACHI OF BRUGGE WAS THE FIRST PLAYER TO SCORE A GOAL IN THE MODERN DAY FORMAT OF THE CHAMPIONS LEAGUE IN 1992.

GOALKEEPER PETER SCHMEICHEL PLAYED FOR BOTH MANCHESTER UNITED AND MANCHESTER CITY, AND NEVER FINISHED ON THE LOSING SIDE IN ALL OF THE DERBY MATCHES BETWEEN THEM.

WEST BROMWICH ALBION WERE THE FIRST TEAM TO WIN THE FA CUP AND THE OLD DIVISION 1 TITLE IN THE SAME YEAR.

ENGLAND AND MANCHESTER UNITED DEFENDER RIO FERDINAND INJURED HIS KNEE IN 2007 WHILST WATCHING TV WITH HIS FEET UP.

ANTONIO CABRINI WAS THE FIRST PLAYER EVER TO MISS A PENALTY IN A WORLD CUP FINAL MATCH IN 1982.

THE 2000 CHAMPIONS LEAGUE FINAL BETWEEN REAL MADRID AND VALENCIA WAS THE FIRST FINAL TO FEATURE TWO TEAMS FROM THE SAME COUNTRY.

JOSE BATISTA OF URUGUAY HOLDS THE RECORD FOR THE QUICKEST WORLD CUP SENDING OFF — HE LASTED LESS THAN A MINUTE IN A GAME AGAINST SCOTLAND.

THE EUROPEAN CHAMPIONSHIP TROPHY WAS MADE LARGER IN 2008, AND THE MARBLE PLINTH IT USED TO STAND ON WAS REMOVED. THE WINNING TEAMS' NAMES ARE NOW ENGRAVED ON THE BACK OF THE TROPHY RATHER THAN ON THE PLINTH.

100,000 TURNED UP TO THE FUNERAL OF NORTHERN IRELAND LEGEND GEORGE BEST IN 2005.

THE OLDEST PLAYER EVER TO SCORE A GOAL AT THE WORLD CUP FINALS WAS ROGER MILLA, WHO SCORED FOR CAMEROON AGAINST RUSSIA IN 1994 AT THE AGE OF 42.

MARSEILLE WERE STRIPPED OF THEIR 1993 EUROPEAN TITLE AFTER A DOMESTIC MATCH-FIXING SCANDAL.

AUSTRIA BEAT SWITZERLAND 7-5 IN THE 1954 WORLD CUP FINALS.

STOKE CITY STARTED THE SECOND HALF OF THEIR 1902 MATCH AGAINST LIVERPOOL WITH JUST SEVEN PLAYERS, AS THE REST FELL VICTIM TO FOOD POISONING FROM A PRE-MATCH MEAL.

SCOTTISH LEGEND KENNY DALGLISH WAS THE FIRST PLAYER EVER TO SCORE 100 GOALS IN BOTH THE SCOTTISH AND ENGLISH TOP DIVISIONS.

THE 1973 FA CUP FINAL WAS THE ONLY ONE TO DATE IN WHICH AN ORANGE BALL WAS USED.

IN THE FIRST EVER WORLD CUP FINAL IN 1930, THE BALL HAD TO BE CHANGED AT HALF-TIME BECAUSE OF A DISPUTE BETWEEN URUGUAY AND ARGENTINA.

MANCHESTER UNITED'S ORIGINAL COLOURS WERE YELLOW AND GREEN.

GERMAN FRANZ BECKENBAUER WAS THE FIRST MAN TO WIN WORLD CUPS AS BOTH A CAPTAIN AND A TEAM MANAGER.

SCOTTISH SIDE SELKIRK WERE ONCE HAMMERED 20-0 BY STIRLING ALBION IN A SCOTTISH CUP MATCH (1984).

BRAZILIAN STAR RONALDO HAS SCORED MORE WORLD CUP FINALS GOALS THAN ANY OTHER PLAYER (15).

ARSENAL LEGEND CHARLIE GEORGE WORKED AS A PUB LANDLORD AND A MECHANIC AFTER RETIRING FROM FOOTBALL.

THE FA CHARITY SHIELD EVOLVED FROM THE SHERIFF OF LONDON SHIELD FIXTURE THAT WAS PLAYED ANNUALLY BETWEEN A PROFESSIONAL TEAM AND A LEADING AMATEUR TEAM.

MANCHESTER UNITED WON JUST FIVE GAMES IN THE CHAMPIONS LEAGUE IN 1998/99, YET WENT ON TO LIFT THE TROPHY.

FULHAM'S SEAN DAVIS IS THE ONLY PLAYER TO HAVE PLAYED IN THE ENGLISH PREMIERSHIP, CHAMPIONSHIP, DIVISION 1 AND DIVISION 2 FOR THE SAME CLUB.

POLAND'S ERNST WILLIMOWSKI SCORED FOUR GOALS IN A SINGLE WORLD CUP GAME AND STILL ENDED UP ON THE LOSING SIDE.

AN ANGRY MOB OF ARGENTINES STORMED THE URUGUAYAN EMBASSY AFTER URUGUAY BEAT ARGENTINA IN THE FIRST WORLD CUP FINAL.

GARY ABLETT IS THE ONLY PLAYER TO HAVE WON THE FA CUP WITH BOTH LIVERPOOL AND EVERTON.

TOM HANKS AND OZZY OSBOURNE ARE BOTH FANS OF ASTON VILLA.

RAUL IS THE CHAMPIONS LEAGUE'S RECORD GOAL SCORER, WITH 60 GOALS IN TOTAL.

CARLOS CASZELY OF CHILE BECAME THE FIRST PLAYER TO BE SENT OFF DURING A WORLD CUP FINAL TOURNAMENT GAME IN 1974.

URUGUAY ARE THE ONLY REIGNING WORLD CUP HOLDERS NOT TO DEFEND THEIR TITLE.

THE EUROPEAN CHAMPIONSHIP TROPHY IS CALLED THE HENRI DELAUNAY TROPHY IN MEMORY OF THE FIRST GENERAL SECRETARY OF UEFA, WHO CAME UP WITH THE IDEA.

INDONESIAN INTERNATIONAL FOOTBALLER MISTAR WAS KILLED BY WILD PIGS WHICH STAMPEDED THROUGH HIS TEAM'S TRAINING PITCH BEFORE A 1995 WORLD CUP MATCH.

CHELSEA FC WERE FORMED AT THE RISING SUN PUB IN FULHAM, LONDON.

GEOFF HURST BECAME THE FIRST PLAYER TO SCORE A HAT TRICK IN A WORLD CUP FINAL IN 1966.

UKRAINE WILL MAKE THEIR DEBUT AT THE EUROPEAN CHAMPIONSHIPS IN 2012, AS JOINT HOSTS (WITH POLAND).

TEN OF THE SIXTEEN TEAMS THAT MADE THE FIFTH ROUND OF THE 2008 FA CUP PLAYED OUTSIDE OF THE ENGLISH TOP DIVISION.

THE FIRST ENGLISH PREMIERSHIP MANAGER TO PART COMPANY WITH HIS TEAM IN THE 2007/2008 SEASON WAS CHELSEA'S JOSE MOURINHO.

THE 1982 WORLD CUP WAS THE FIRST TO FEATURE A PENALTY SHOOT OUT.

THE FIRST SCOTTISH SIDE TO FACE ENGLAND AT THE KENNINGTON OVAL INCLUDED THREE LONDON-BASED PLAYERS BECAUSE THE SCOTTISH INTERNATIONAL FUND COULD ONLY STRETCH TO PAYING EIGHT RETURN TRAIN TICKETS.

GERMAN GERD MULLER WAS THE FIRST PLAYER TO WIN THE WORLD CUP GOLDEN BOOT TWICE.

NEWCASTLE AND ENGLAND LEGEND ALAN SHEARER ONLY EVER WON ONE TITLE – THE PREMIERSHIP TITLE IN 1994/1995 WITH BLACKBURN.

LIVERPOOL CAME FROM 3-0 DOWN AT HALF-TIME TO DEFEAT MILAN ON PENALTIES IN THE 2005 CHAMPIONS LEAGUE FINAL.

REFEREE KEN ASTON INVENTED THE SYSTEM OF RED AND YELLOW CARDS WHILE WAITING AT A SET OF TRAFFIC LIGHTS. THEY WERE INTRODUCED INTO THE WORLD CUP IN 1970.

A GAME BETWEEN DERBY AND SUNDERLAND IN 1894 FEATURED THREE HALVES, AFTER THE OFFICIAL REFEREE TURNED UP AT HALF TIME AND ORDERED THE FIRST HALF TO BE PLAYED AGAIN.

IRAN BEAT THE MALDIVES 17-0 IN A 1998 WORLD CUP QUALIFYING GAME.

ARSENAL WERE FIRST PROMOTED TO THE TOP DIVISION IN ENGLAND IN 1919.

IN THE VERY FIRST EUROPEAN CHAMPIONSHIP IN 1960, SPAIN WITHDREW FROM THEIR QUARTER FINAL MATCH AGAINST THE USSR ON POLITICAL GROUNDS. THE USSR WENT ON TO WIN THE COMPETITION.

THE UNITED STATES REACHED THE WORLD CUP FINALS IN 1990 AFTER AN ABSENCE OF FORTY YEARS.

SIR BOBBY CHARLTON OF ENGLAND ONLY FOUND OUT THAT HE HAD BEEN BOOKED IN A 1966 MATCH AGAINST ARGENTINA 32 YEARS AFTER THE GAME.

CARDIFF CITY ARE THE ONLY NON-ENGLISH TEAM TO EVER WIN THE FA CUP.

THE FIRST EVER WORLD CUP WAS HOSTED BY URUGUAY IN 1930. URUGUAY WERE ALSO THE FIRST WINNERS.

THE RECORD FOR THE HIGHEST SCORING MATCH IN ENGLISH PREMIER LEAGUE HISTORY WAS BROKEN ON 29TH SEPTEMBER 2007 WHEN PORTSMOUTH BEAT READING 7-4.

AZERBAIJAN HAD TO PLAY ALL THEIR 1996 EUROPEAN CHAMPIONSHIP HOME GAMES IN TURKEY DUE TO A CIVIL WAR RAGING IN THEIR OWN COUNTRY.

ZAIRE REPLACED THEIR GOALKEEPER AFTER JUST 22 MINUTES OF ONE WORLD CUP FINALS GAME — HE HAD ALREADY CONCEDED THREE GOALS BY THIS TIME.

THE FA CUP WAS INVENTED BY CW ALCOCK IN 1871 — AND HE ALSO CAPTAINED THE FIRST SIDE TO WIN IT IN 1872.

ARGENTINA REFUSED TO SEND THEIR BEST PLAYERS TO THE 1934 WORLD CUP FINALS IN ITALY BECAUSE THEY WERE SCARED THEY WOULD DEFECT.

THE 1911 CHARITY SHIELD FINAL WAS THE HIGHEST SCORING, WITH MANCHESTER UNITED BEATING SWINDON 8-4.

AL DIBA SCORED ALL FOUR GOALS IN THE FINAL OF THE FIRST AFRICA CUP OF NATIONS, AS EGYPT BEAT ETHIOPIA 4-0.

ITALY WERE THE FIRST TEAM TO RETAIN THE WORLD CUP, IN 1938.

OSCAR ALFREDO COX ORGANISED THE FIRST FOOTBALL MATCH IN BRAZIL IN 1901, AFTER FOUR YEARS OF TRYING TO GET BRAZILIANS TO TAKE AN INTEREST IN THE GAME.

REAL MADRID WON THE FIRST EVER EUROPEAN CUP FINAL IN 1956 — AND THE NEXT FOUR, TOO.

THE ONLY WORLD CUP FINALS NOT DECIDED BY A ONE MATCH FINAL WERE THE 1950 FINALS, WON BY BRAZIL.

ITALIAN PLAYER FRANCESCO TOTTI WAS GIVEN A THREE-MATCH BAN FOR SPITTING AT THE EURO 2004 CHAMPIONSHIPS.

THE UEFA CUP WAS PREVIOUSLY KNOWN AS THE INTER-CITY FAIRS CUP.

AT THE 1982 WORLD CUP FINALS AUSTRIA AND WEST GERMANY PLAYED OUT A FARCICAL MATCH IN WHICH BOTH TEAMS JUST KICKED THE BALL AROUND AIMLESSLY AFTER GERMANY TOOK A 1-0 LEAD IN THE TENTH MINUTE. THE RESULT ENSURED THAT BOTH TEAMS QUALIFIED.

COLOMBIA WERE CHOSEN TO BE THE HOSTS FOR THE 1986 WORLD CUP FINALS, BUT DECIDED THEY COULDN'T AFFORD TO HOST THE EVENT AND SO IT WAS HELD IN MEXICO INSTEAD.

ABIDE WITH ME WAS FIRST SUNG AT THE FA CUP FINAL IN 1927.

IN THE 1947/1948 SEASON, BOTH MANCHESTER TEAMS PLAYED THEIR HOME GAMES AT THE SAME STADIUM, MAINE ROAD.

JIMMY GREAVES HAD TO CATCH A STRAY DOG DURING ENGLAND'S 1962 WORLD CUP GAME AGAINST BRAZIL.

THE 2008 UEFA CUP SAW TEAMS FROM MONTENEGRO COMPETE FOR THE FIRST TIME.

THE FIRST FOOTBALLER EVER TO BE KNIGHTED WAS SIR STANLEY MATTHEWS.

THE MATCH BETWEEN FRANCE AND HUNGARY AT THE 1978 WORLD CUP WAS DELAYED WHEN BOTH TEAMS TURNED UP WEARING VERY SIMILAR KITS. THE FRENCH HAD TO BORROW THE KIT OF THE LOCAL ARGENTINE TEAM, KIMBERLEY FC.

BRAZILIAN WORLD CUP LEGEND SOCRATES FAILED TO MAKE IT INTO IRISH TEAM SHELBOURNE'S SQUAD WHEN HE WAS A MEDICAL STUDENT IN DUBLIN.

FAMOUS ANTIGUAN CRICKETER VIV RICHARDS ALSO PLAYED FOR HIS NATIONAL FOOTBALL TEAM DURING THE 1974 WORLD CUP QUALIFYING CAMPAIGN.

THE 1970 WORLD CUP FINALS WERE THE FIRST TO ALLOW THE USE OF SUBSTITUTES.

THE FIRST EVER SCOTTISH LEAGUE PRODUCED JOINT WINNERS FOR THE ONLY TIME IN ITS HISTORY. RANGERS AND DUMBARTON FINISHED ON THE SAME POINTS AND THEN PLAYED A PLAY-OFF MATCH WHICH THEY DREW 2-2.

IN 2038 THERE WILL NO LONGER BE ROOM FOR THE WINNING TEAMS' NAMES ON THE EXISTING WORLD CUP TROPHY.

IN 1909 THE ENGLISH FA REFUSED TO SEND ANY TEAM TO THE SIR THOMAS LIPTON TROPHY IN ITALY, AN EARLY INTERNATIONAL TOUR-NAMENT. AS A RESULT, THE ORGANISERS INVITED WEST AUCKLAND FC, AN AMATEUR SIDE COMPRISED MAINLY OF COAL MINERS. THEY WON, AND SUCCESSFULLY DEFENDED THEIR TITLE IN 1911 TOO.

IN 1963, TOTTENHAM HOTSPUR BECAME THE FIRST ENGLISH CLUB TO WIN A MAJOR EUROPEAN TROPHY.